HOW THINGS HAVE CHANGED

In the
Home

Jon Richards

Chrysalis Education

Distributed in the United States by
Smart Apple Media
2140 Howard Drive West
North Mankato, Minnesota 56003

Library of Congress Control Number: 20041108648

ISBN 1-59389-198-9

Editorial Manager: Joyce Bentley
Editorial Assistant: Camilla Lloyd
Produced by Tall Tree Ltd.
Designer: Ed Simkins
Editor: Kate Simkins
Consultant: Jon Kirkwood
Picture Researcher: Lorna Ainger

Printed in China.

Some of the more unfamiliar words used in this book
are explained in the glossary on page 31.

Photo Credits:
The publishers would like to thank the following for
their kind permission to reproduce the photographs:

Lorna Ainger: 21b, 23b, 28t, 29c
AKG Images: Bibliotheque Nationale, Paris 8
Alamy.com: Ginsberg 4, Martine Hamilton Knight/Arcaid 7t,
Robert Harding World Imagery 14, Justin Kase 5b, 28bl
Art Archive: Bibliotheque des Arts Decoratifs,
Paris/Dagli Orti 22
Courtesy Baxi Potterton/Baxi Heating UK Ltd.: 9t
Corbis: Bettmann 10, 25tr, FC br, William Gottlieb 21t, BC,
Historical Picture Archive 12, Michael Nicholson 24, Galen
Rowell 6, 30, FC tl
Digital Vision: 7b

Courtesy Dolphin Bathrooms: 2, 23t, FC c
Courtesy Electrolux (Timeline): 1, 15b, 17b
Getty: Hulton Archive 13b, 18, 19cl, 20, 29bl, MPI 11t, David
Silverman 9, Yoshikazu Tsuno 25l, Adrian Ace Williams 15t
Courtesy LG Electronics: 26, 27t, 29tr, FC bl
Robert Opie: 16
OSRAM Limited: 19r, 31
Rex Features Ltd.: Voisin/Phanie 13t
Science Photo Library: Alex Bartel 5t
Still Pictures: Martin Bond 27b
Tall Tree Ltd.: 11b, 17t, 29br, FC tr

Contents

Building methods

T he need for shelter is one of our most basic requirements. Since people first started to build their own homes around 12,000 BC, the materials and methods used to construct homes have changed greatly.

The earliest homes were either natural shelters or tents. However, as people started to settle in one place, more permanent homes, made from stronger materials, such as wood, mud, or stone, were needed.

▼ Many medieval home such as this one, were bu with a visible wooden framework, which was fil in with mud and dung.

◀ *Today, concrete is poured around thick bars of iron or steel to make a structure that is strong. This is called reinforced concrete.*

EUREKA!

In about 4000 BC, the people of Ancient Mesopotamia made the first oven-dried bricks. They mixed mud with clay and baked the bricks hard inside a special fire, called a kiln. Bricks are still a commonly used building material.

The Romans started to use concrete to make buildings around 200 BC, and they were also the first people to use clear glass in their homes to let in light. Today, many modern materials are used to construct homes, including plastic and fiberglass.

All shapes and sizes

As the range of materials used in house construction has increased and the needs of people have changed, so the size and shape of the homes we live in has altered. This has created a great variety of homes around the world.

In the ancient world, particularly in poorer homes or colder climates, families lived, ate, and slept in single-room buildings. Houses with many rooms, such as Roman villas, were for the wealthy or for those living in hot countries where they didn't need to huddle together to keep warm.

▼ The earliest peoples were nomads. They carr their homes, usually tents, with them. Today, some noma such as these peop in China, live in modern as well as traditional tents.

Modern Western houses are usually built with more than one story and with many rooms for different purposes, such as sleeping, eating, and bathing.

Today, homes vary from simple huts to large mansions with many rooms. The type of home people choose depends on where they live, the number of people living there, and the climate. The cost and the availability of building materials are also important.

EUREKA!

The invention of the safety elevator in 1853 by Elisha Otis was an important step in building development. It provided a safe way of climbing many stories quickly and was one of the main reasons that very tall buildings, such as skyscrapers, became possible.

Keeping warm

Humans started to use fire to keep warm nearly 1.5 million years ago. Open fires remained the main way to heat home until the 19th century, when central heating became popula

In the earliest buildings, an open fire was positioned in the middle of a room and people gathered around it to stay warm. Smoke would leave through a hole in the middle of the roof.

◄ Chimneys were first built into homes in medieval Europe. The smoke from the fireplace traveled up a flue, or channel, in the wall. It then exited the building via a chimney stack on the roof.

In the 19th century, the need to heat large factories led to the development of central heating. Today, the most common types of central heating use either warm air or hot water. Warm air is released from ducts into the house. Hot water travels in pipes to metal radiators that then give off heat.

◄ The air or water in a central-heating system is heated by burning fuel, such as gas. Most western homes have water heaters called boilers.

EUREKA!

One of the earliest forms of central heating was developed by the Romans. Known as a hypocaust, it used fire to warm the air. The hot air flowed through spaces beneath the floor, heating the rooms above. The remains of a hypocaust are shown here.

Cooking at home

People have been cooking food for thousands of years to mak
it safe to eat and better tasting. Many cooking methods have
been developed, from the open fire to electric ovens.

The earliest forms of
cooking involved heating
food over an open fire.
Around 2000 BC, the
Ancient Egyptians
became the first peop
to bake food, such a
bread, in clay ovens.

◀ *Fires were used to cook
food by our ancestors many
thousands of years ago.*

The first cooking ranges were introduced in the 1780s. They were made up of an open fire with an oven and burners on each side. The first electric oven was installed in a hotel in 1889. Most modern ovens are heated by electricity or gas. Some contain fans that circulate the hot air to make the food cook more quickly and evenly.

▲ *Cooking ranges, such as this one from the 19th century, included burners on which pots and pans were placed to boil or fry food and ovens in which food was roasted or baked.*

LOOK CLOSER

The microwave oven was invented by Percy Spencer in 1946. It works by producing a high-energy field that causes tiny molecules inside food to vibrate. This vibration creates the heat that cooks the food. Microwave ovens cook food in less time than ordinary ovens.

Keeping food

For thousands of years, people have been preserving food to make it last longer. This meant that food could be stored in t home for future use. Today, most modern homes have refrigerators or freezers to keep food fresh.

▲ Food, such as fish or meat, was hung in a smoke house, where smoke from a fire was used to preserve the food.

The Sumerians, whose civilization flourished around 3000 BC, were the first people to dry and smoke fish to preserve it. Another early storage method, called pickling, used a salty liquid or vinegar to preserve food.

◄ In a refrigerator, food can be kept fresh for a long time. This means people do not have to buy new produce every day.

round 1000 BC, the Chinese were one of e first people to keep food fresh by keeping in snow stored in their cellars. Ice was used ice boxes and ice houses to keep food esh until the middle of the 19th century. hen, in 1834, American Jacob Perkins vented the refrigerator.

EUREKA!

After spending time in Canada as a fur trader, Clarence Birdseye noticed how local people there froze food in the ice to preserve it. He brought this technique back with him to the US. In 1929, he introduced the first freezer and started to sell frozen foods.

Washing clothes

Keeping clothes clean has always required a lot of effort. The development of washing machines in the 1800s meant that what once took all day could now be done in a few hours.

The earliest records of washing clothes dates back to Ancient Egypt around 3500 BC. From then until the the 19th century, the method of washing clothes changed very little, relying largely on pounding and scrubbing clothes by hand to clean them.

▼ Traditional meth of washing clothes still used in many p of the world today.

The first powdered soap was introduced in 1843. Before then people had used clay, animal fat, and even urine to help clean clothes. Many machines have been invented to make the hard work of doing the laundry easier. They include the washing machine and, in 1909, the tumble drier.

◀ *Early washing devices included the washboard. The ridges meant that clothes could be thoroughly scrubbed.*

EUREKA!

In 1851, James King invented a hand-operated washing machine with a spinning drum that pounded the clothes together to remove dirt. The first electric washing machine, designed by Alva Fisher in 1907, also had a drum, as do most modern machines.

Housecleaning

The invention of vacuum cleaners revolutionized housework. They replaced traditional methods of cleaning, such as beating and sweeping, which were tiring and messy, and they made it quicker and easier to get rid of dirt.

The DOOM of the DUSTER the BRUSH and the BROOM

THE ASPIRATOR

CLEANS EVERYTHING BY AIR SUCTION

Many different tools have been used to clean homes over the years, including beaters, brushes, brooms, and feather dusters. Little changed in the design of housecleaning tools until the start of the 20th century.

◄ *This early, hand-operated vacuum cleaner sucked up dirt, but it was heavy and awkward to move around.*

Some modern vacuum cleaners do not need to use bags to collect dust. Instead, air and dust are sucked up from the floor and spun very quickly. This spinning flings any dust to one side, where it is collected in a plastic cylinder that can be emptied when full and used again.

▼ *Modern vacuum cleaners are designed to be light and easy to use. Many have disposable bags to collect the dust.*

In 1901, Hubert Booth showed that you could suck dirt out of a seat and into a handkerchief. He went on to invent the vacuum cleaner. Portable vacuum cleaners were developed by William Henry Hoover in 1926. They used brushes to beat the carpet and an electric pump to suck the dirt up into a bag.

Light in the home

The development of lighting in the home meant that people were able to carry out activities that previously could only be done during the day.

The earliest lights were simple oil lamps made by cave dwellers from hollowed out stones around 40,000 BC. Other early forms of light included burning torches or candles. Although dim by modern standards, these early lights still allowed people to work and play after the sun had set.

▼ Oil lamps, such as this one from the 18th century, could produce enoug light to read a book by.

EUREKA!

In trying to invent the world's first lightbulb, Thomas Edison tried many different materials, including platinum and human hair. The problem was in finding a filament that could glow without burning out. In the summer of 1880, Edison discovered that fibers of carbonized bamboo made the best filaments for a bulb.

the 18th century, homes began to be lit ith gas, providing a constant and reliable urce of light. The gas, usually coal gas, was ped into homes and burned in lamps. ith the invention of the lightbulb, gas was placed by electricity, allowing people to light dark room at the flick of a switch.

OSRAM DULUX EL
20W/41-827 · 220-240V
50/60Hz · Made in Germany

▲ *Many modern lightbulbs are designed to last a long time and to be energy efficient.*

Entertainment

Amusements in the home have changed over the years, from storytelling and playing music to radio, television, and, more recently, computer games.

Traditional forms of household entertainment were usually performed by family members who would sing songs and play games. The first entertainment machine appeared in 1877, when Thomas Edison invented the phonograph, an early type of record player.

◀ Victorian famil would often gathe in the parlor to listen to music.

he first radio signal was transmitted in 1895 by
alian Guglielmo Marconi, but it was not until 1920
at regular radio broadcasts started. Small portable
dios for the home appeared soon after. Then, in
)28, the first regular television service started,
aming pictures into people's homes for the first time.

▲ *Radio and, later, television brought entertainment, news, and information from the studio or theater into a family's living room.*

LOOK CLOSER

Since John Logie Baird invented the television in 1924, it has become a central feature in many homes around the world. In 2001, there were 248 million television sets in the US alone, with 98.2 percent of households owning at least one. The average number of TVs was 2.4 per household.

In the bathroom

Since ancient times, people have bathed or showered to clean themselves. Regular bathing, however, was only possible for the rich. The introduction of plumbing into homes in the 20th century meant that ordinary people were able to wash dail

Ancient peoples placed great importance on staying clean, although often it was only the rich who could afford to do so. Ruins from Ancient Egypt, Greece, and Rome include special public bathrooms, bathhouses, and pools.

◄ A visit to a Roman bathhouse involved steaming, cleaning, and massaging the body. Famous Roman baths include the baths of Caracalla in Rome.

▲ *Modern homes often have an indoor bathroom with a bathtub and shower combined.*

rivate bathrooms did not become popular ntil the development of plumbing and heap fuel to heat the water. Before then, ashing was done in wooden or metal tubs ith water heated on a fire.

EUREKA!

Soap was developed around 500 BC. The Phoenicians used a mixture of goat's fat and wood ashes to wash themselves. The Celts of Britain also used a mixture of animal fat and plant ashes, calling it *saipo*, from which the modern name comes.

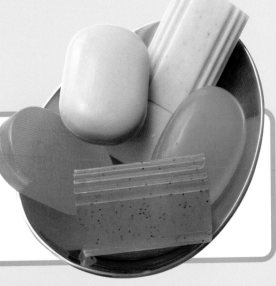

Toilets

One problem with having so many homes close together was what to do with the human waste that was created. If it's not removed safely, sewage becomes a foul-smelling problem that can cause disease.

The earliest toilets discovered belonged to the Indus civilization of Asia. They had simple brick lavatories with seats that opened into a cesspool or drain. Although many civilizations built toilets, the main problem was developing a sewage system to get rid of the waste.

▼ The Romans built public toilets with ho carved into stone seats, such as these from Ephesus in Turkey, which was p of the Roman Empire

EUREKA!

Important dates marking the development of the toilet include: 1596, Sir John Harrington published a design for a flushing toilet; 1775, Alexander Cummings patented the S-shaped bend to trap bad smells; and 1884, Thomas Crapper's valveless cistern meant toilets could flush efficiently.

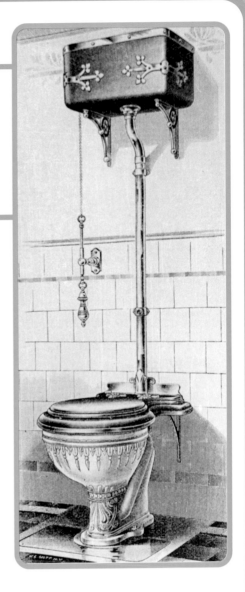

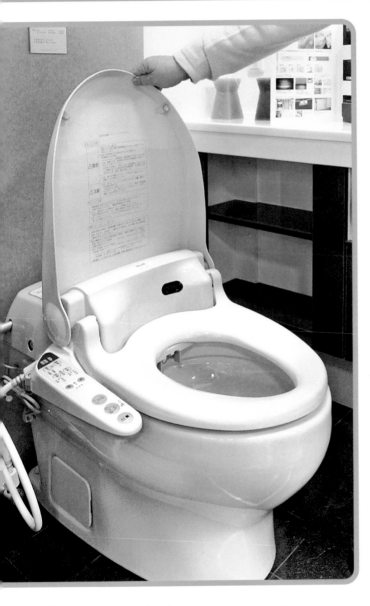

This ultramodern toilet from Japan contains seat warmer and an air freshener.

Without a system of carrying sewage away safely, diseases, such as cholera and typhoid, were common. It was not until the 19th century that people understood the connection between sewage and disease and started to build systems that could carry waste away.

The future home

With all the modern devices in our homes today, how can things possibly improve? Well, inventors are looking for ways to make the places we live in even easier to take care of and kinder to the environment.

The development of the computer in the 20th century led to the creation of machines that can perform boring tasks, such as cleaning. With more parents at work, this means people can spend less time on household chores and more time relaxing.

◀ *This refrigerator is linked to the Internet and can order food automatically from suppliers when stocks run low.*

One of the latest developments will be the introduction of the Internet into homes. Electrical systems in a home will be connected to the Internet and controlled via any online computer. This will make it possible for people to turn on lights, heating, or the oven before they return home!

The latest vacuum cleaners e robots. The machines ntain computers that guide em around a room, cleaning entirely on their own.

LOOK CLOSER

Heating and lighting our homes is expensive and causes pollution. New, cleaner ways of supplying energy are being tried. These include solar power, which uses special panels to change the sun's rays into electricity. Solar energy doesn't pollute the atmosphere.

Timeline

- c.12,000 BC. The first homes are built.

- c.8000 BC. The first towns and cities are established.

- c.500 BC. The Phoenicians develop the first soap.

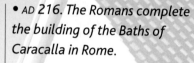

- AD 216. The Romans complete the building of the Baths of Caracalla in Rome.

- c.2000 BC. The Ancient Egyptians use clay ovens to bake food.

- c.1780. The first cooking ranges are introduced.

12,000 BC

- c.1000 BC. The Chinese use snow to keep food cold in cellars.

- 1834. Jacob Perk invents the refrigerato

- 1843. The first powdered soap for clothes is introduced

- c.3000 BC. Earliest evidence of candles from Ancient Egyptian candlesticks.

- c.200 BC. The Romans use concrete to construct buildings.

- c.3000 BC. The Ancient Sumerians dry and smoke their food to preserve it.

- 1775. Alexander Cummings patent the S-bend in toile

- 1596. Sir John Harrington designs the first flushing toilet.

- c.4000 BC. Bricks are invented in Mesopotamia.

• 1851. *James King develops the first washing machine with a spinning drum.*

• 1853. *Elisha Otis develops the safety elevator.*

• 1884. *Thomas Crapper develops the valveless water cistern.*

• 1907. *Alva Fisher designs the first electric washing machine.*

• 1909. *The first electric tumble driers are introduced.*

• 1920. *The world's first commercial radio station starts broadcasting.*

• 1924. *John Logie Baird invents the television.*

• 1926. *William Henry Hoover creates the first practical household vacuum cleaner.*

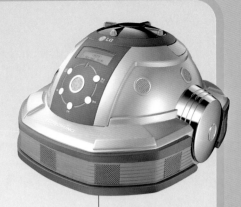

• 2003. *Robot vacuum cleaners are available for the first time.*

TODAY

• 1901. *Hubert Booth demonstrates how vacuum cleaning could work.*

• 1895. *The first radio signal is transmitted by Guglielmo Marconi.*

• c.1970. *The first home video games are sold.*

• 1946. *Percy Spencer invents the microwave oven.*

• 1929. *Clarence Birdseye sells frozen food.*

• 1880. *Thomas Edison develops a working lightbulb.*

Factfile

• Concrete was invented by the Romans, who mixed volcanic ash with water, lime, and stone fragments to form a material that was rocklike when dry.

• The largest home that is not a palace is St. Emmeram Castle in Regensburg, Germany. It has 517 rooms.

• The Roman Baths of Caracalla in Rome were some of the largest baths built in the empire. They could hold up to 1,600 bathers at one time.

• The tallest residential building in the world is the Trump Tower in New York City, with 72 stories.

• The average adult spends 1,670 hours watching the television each year—that the equivalent of 70 whole days!

• Candles are some of the earliest inventions known. This has been shown by the discovery of candlesticks from Ancient Crete and Egypt that date back to 3000 BC.

Glossary

...iler

...machine that heats water. The hot water ...en pumped through pipes and ...iators around a home as part of a central ...ting system.

...tern

...ank for storing ...ter. A small cistern ...onnected to a toilet ...store the water used ...flushing.

...ncrete

...building material made ...t of cement, sand, stone, ...d water that can be ...ured when it is wet and ...es to form a hard material.

...ament

...coil of wire that is found at ...center of a lightbulb. It ...ws brightly when an electrical ...rrent flows through it.

...dus civilization

...civilization that flourished about ...000 years ago in what is now ...odern Pakistan.

...esopotamia

...region of the Middle East situated in what ...now modern Iraq that was the site of several ...cient civilizations.

Nomad

A person who moves around from place to place in search of food and water.

Patent

This is official recognition that an inventor is the only person who can make, use, and sell a device.

Phoenicians

An ancient culture that existed about 3,000 years ago in what is now the countries of Lebanon, Syria, and Israel.

Plumbing

A network of pipes that circulate water around the house.

Preserve

To stop food from rotting by using methods such as freezing.

Sewage

Waste matter from homes and factories that is carried away in sewers and drains to water-treatment plants. There it is cleaned before being released into streams and rivers.

Sumer

An ancient culture that flourished about 6,500 years ago in modern Iraq.

Index